D1461847

IAIN SINCLAIR was born in 1943 in Cardiff, Wales and studied at Trinity College, Dublin, and the Courtauld Institute, London. A renowned essayist and writer of fiction, his early work consisted mostly of poetry, which he published on his own small press, Albion Village Press. He has written and presented a number of films and has co-directed with Chris Petit four documentaries for Channel 4, one of which, *Asylum*, won the short film prize at the Montreal Festival. He was also the editor of the Paladin Poetry Series. His book *Downriver* won the James Tait Black Memorial Prize and the Encore Award, and he has since produced many books including: *Radon Daughters*; *Lights Out for the Territory*; *London Orbital*; *Edge of the Orison*; *London: City of Disappearances*, (ed.); and *Hackney, That Rose-Red Empire: A Confidential Report*. For the Swedenborg Society he has written *Blake's London: the Topographic Sublime* (2011) and, with Brian Catling, *Several Clouds Colliding* co-published with BookWorks. His most recent book *Living with Buildings: And Walking with Ghosts* was published in 2018.

SWIMMING TO HEAVEN: THE LOST RIVERS OF LONDON is the second in a series of Swedenborg Archive pocket books. Edited by Stephen McNeilly and drawing on miscellaneous material and other ephemera from the Swedenborg archives, the aim of the pocket book series is to make available, in printed form, lectures, interviews and other unique items that would otherwise remain unseen by a broader audience.

Swimming to Heaven:
the Lost Rivers of London

Swimming to Heaven:
the Lost Rivers of London

IAIN SINCLAIR

The Swedenborg Society
20-21 Bloomsbury Way
London
WC1A 2TH

2018

Series editor: Stephen McNeilly

Typeset at Swedenborg House.
Printed at T J International, Padstow.
Cover and book design © Stephen McNeilly
Original text transcribed by Alex Murray

Published by:
The Swedenborg Society
Swedenborg House
20-21 Bloomsbury Way
London WC1A 2TH

ISBN : 978-0-85448-179-8
British Library Cataloguing-in-Publication Data.
A catalogue record for this book
is available from the British Library.

Contents

Preliminary note

Swimming to Heaven: the Lost Rivers of London,
by Iain Sinclair, is a revised transcript of a talk given
at Barnard's Inn Hall, Holborn on Monday 22 June
2009 entitled 'London's Lost Rivers: The Hackney
Brook and other North West Passages'. Organized by
Gresham College as part of the programme for the
City of London Festival the talk lasted around an
hour and explored the theme of London's lost rivers
as underlying narratives and erasures of the city.

The text published here, containing new material
and a new title, has undergone substantial revision
and can best be considered a new work (with the
original transcript serving as a 'memory prompt' or
'structural model'). Passages exploring the relation

between William Blake and Swedenborg have been extended and elaborated, with Swedenborg's famous 'mud baptism' of 1744 emerging as a central and defining motif. As with other volumes in the Swedenborg Archive series, citations have been referenced as endnotes.

Readers familiar with the broader framework of Iain's work will recognize the parallels with *Hackney, That Rose-Red Empire*, published concurrently with Iain's original talk at Gresham College. Similarly those interested in the sections on Swedenborg and Blake may wish to explore *Blake's London: The Topographic Sublime*—the first in this series of pocket Swedenborg archive books—to which this volume can be viewed as a companion or counterpoint.

Stephen McNeilly

Swimming to Heaven:
the Lost Rivers of London

H ere is a warning, just to put you into the right frame of mind——my talk is the equivalent of a swim in murky waters, sometimes floating under the stars, sometimes thrashing against the current, sometimes beached and gasping. I love water and the parts of us that are water. And I love the people who come at the end of a day to some bench or perch overlooking the great fact of the sea. I think of the poet Charles Olson, especially; a giant of a man marooned in Gloucester, Massachusetts, contemplating the immensity of the problem he has set himself, the requirement to take his epic, *The Maximus Poems*, [1] out there towards the origin, the mountain ranges beneath the Atlantic, and then to bring the story back to land, to the oldest myths and to the holiness of the heart's affections. Jeremy Prynne, talking about this poem, describes the coast as 'that ambiguous delicate line between the land and the sea, with its prime sexual ambiguity'. [2]

Olson, as a young boy, staying at a summer cottage, walks down to the place where two old men sit smoking and talking. It's a pivotal moment for him. You can't help feeling the immensity, the reach of the land behind, with that overriding impulse to counter it, by watching the shifts and shimmies of the sea. There are no answers and there are not even any proper questions. The voices of two old working men talking, gossiping, telling tales, remembering. It is exactly as Prynne calls it. 'You take what has been *story* and you fold it back into *legend*.' [2]

Olson believed that the World had become divided from the Universe. And that's what, tramping around London, or out at the rough

edges, I have come to feel too. Swimming——
immersion, drift——might be one method of
healing this estrangement. Walking over or
alongside the buried rivers of London stitches a
form of collective memory into our sides. That's
why I make the same circuit each morning,
and finish, the rising sun at my back, down a
stretch of the Regent's Canal. And why, when I
was assembling material for my book, *Hackney,
That Rose-Red Empire*,[3] I tried to persuade
Andrew Kötting, the gallivanting filmmaker,
performance artist and cross-Channel swimmer,
to go into the claggy shallows of our local sewer.
I'd walked around the outline of the borough
a number of times, alone, or with various
pressured companions, including Will Self. But
swimming . . . That was something else. Kötting
declined. He didn't know me well enough back
then to trust the register of my madness. Instead,
we circumambulated the water margin, while
he busked, challenged innocent wanderers, and
improvised around his notion of 'desire lines', or

lost paths as sexualized as Olson's coast: tracks stamped out as a means of navigating this new terrain of wired fences, surveillance systems, security guards and suspended permissions.

Years later, the karma of Kötting's initial refusal came back to haunt him. After manoeuvring a swan pedalo, all the way from Hastings, by sea and river, he plunged into the Regent's Canal and swam out from the Stygian darkness of the Islington tunnel. It was a rebirth. Like one of those Old Testament lepers purging their sins by total immersion in the Jordan. Now he was free to return to the South Coast, to continue his challenging all-season catch-tide swims from St Leonards to Bexhill. This is the peculiar English ritual I think of as reverse evolution. Special people, washed up at the end of the land, the end of the possible, contemplating, like Herman Melville, a return to the watery element. The eternal quest. The voyage without end. 'It is a way I have', said Melville's Ishmael, 'of driving off the spleen,

and regulating the circulation'. To submerge,
once again, in the bag of amniotic fluid. To
grow gills. 'All men in their degree, some time
or other, cherish very nearly the same feelings
towards the ocean.' [4]

I told you that we would run against the
tide, taking deep breaths, ducking under the
waves, losing vision. My neurosis persists: the
only ways worth negotiating with this world,
while still hoping to connect with the rhythms
of the cosmos, are by walking and swimming.
Which brings me to the haunting complexity
of London's buried rivers. They're not lost, not
at all. Just because you can't see a thing, as Ed
Dorn points out, doesn't mean that it's not there.
The rivers continue, hidden and culverted as they
might be, to flow through our dreams, fixing
the compass of our moods and movements. The
Walbrook, the Fleet, the Tyburn, the Westbourne,
the Effra, the Neckinger: visible or invisible,
they haunt us. It is not possible to understand
the growth and development of Hackney, for

example, without registering the presence of that subterranean river, the Hackney Brook.

When you write about a place, the first difficulty is finding a way of developing and delivering an adequate mythology. The model for me has always been William Blake. He's a craftsman, a working engraver, a free citizen of these streets. In the background is the disputed connection, through his mother, Catherine, with the Moravian Community known to Swedenborg that's very close to this hall, walking distance, in fact: Fetter Lane. Blake grows up in the shadow of this curious philosophy with which he comes to argue in later life. 'O Swedenborg! Strongest of men, the Samson shorn by the Churches.' [5] In old age, journeying on foot from where he lived close to the Thames, tracking the River Fleet to Hampstead, to visit the Linnells, Blake is making a return to source. He is swimming uphill, absorbing the potency of a partly submerged stream; one of the arteries of his city. There is a very particular sense of London

and its geography. And underlying all of this are
torrential lines of verse in the great epic poems;
wild waters of inspiration surging, stalling,
tumbling over weirs and falls. Blake uses names,
the specific names of modest local places,
and promotes them into his own cosmology.
'Hackney and Holloway sicken.' [6]

As with Blake, so with Swedenborg before him:
rivers. Rivers of memory, of inspiration. Arrival
and departure. Of the passage between life and
death. I come back to the opening sequence of
Our Mutual Friend, the last completed novel by
Charles Dickens; father and daughter out on a
running tide, corpse fishing. Waiting for a dead
man to step ashore, to reclaim a lost life. Their
craft is 'allied to the bottom of the river rather
than the surface, by reason of the slime and ooze
with which it was covered'. What is this affinity
of London visionaries, writers and mystics, with
living water? The original hut settlement and
the walled garrison city, they feel like so much
sediment left behind, or dredged from the broad

Thames. Temporary habitations for intelligent
life forms that fret over business and petty
politics, before submerging once again into the
depths. When the villainous Rogue Riderhood,
once rescued from the river, resuscitated, is on
the point of being hurled from a Lock's edge into
a weir, he says: 'You can't drown Me. Ain't I told
you that a man as has come through drowning
can never be drowned?' [7]

Swedenborg's landfall at Wapping in 1710 is
an anticipation of *Our Mutual Friend*. Like
John Rokesmith, 'The Man from Somewhere', he
comes ashore dead, or under sentence of death,
to enter a period of elective obscurity. To live in
unrecorded lodgings. To walk, read, meditate:
a life in suspension, a season of secret studies.
Biography, being occulted, becomes fiction. The
young, but well-connected Swedish scholar breaks
quarantine. His natural curiosity has him quitting
the plague ship, moving through the downriver
reaches, despite prohibition: a potentially capital
offence. London, allowing him to live, but paying

him no special attention, accepts him as a presence. Troubling episodes of madness, warps of reality, follow. And they are, of course, wide open to misinterpretation, dubious transcripts.

What cannot be set aside is Swedenborg's mud baptism. This is an extraordinary episode from a period, May to July 1744, when he lodges at Salisbury Court, close to the Moravian Church in Fetter Lane. His behaviour, according to contemporary witnesses——John Paul Brockmer, an engraver, and the clergyman, Aron Mathesius, who reports on what Brockmer is alleged to have said——is peculiar, sometimes alarming. 'He lived very recluse.' He would not permit his chamber door to be opened to the maid. He groaned, he wept. His hair stood on end, he foamed at the mouth. Either he was in the grip of a shamanic seizure, afforded overwhelming visions of other worlds, or, by more rational and dimmer explanation, he was undergoing a mental crisis, a breakdown caused by overwork, solitude, a strange city. London, so heavily colonized by the dead, so thick with voices and memory-provoking smells, surging crowds and deserted courts, was the dream. An island fed and sustained by water and its traffic.

What is beyond dispute is that Brockmer suggested Swedenborg's relocation to Warner Street in Cold Bath Fields, to bring his overexcited tenant within reach of a certain Dr Smith. Swedenborg, failing to achieve an audience with the Swedish ambassador, takes to the tight streets, and is reported as stripping himself, flinging his money at the mob, before rolling naked in the deep mud (and worse) of 'a place called the Gully-hole'.[8]

This is the moment I call a baptism. Like so much else in the Swedenborg legend, the incident invites a wide range of interpretation. Is this a simple Scandinavian reflex, a purging and birching in the first convenient puddle in an area of London celebrated for its health-giving springs? Is it a Moravian renunciation of earthly vanities, a making actual of the money-as-shit metaphor? Is it a dreamtime ritual confirming

the potency of the city's songlines? A parable?
Performance art? A strategic provocation?

For the purposes of my watery speculation,
my presentation of London as a liquid city,
alive with the drowned of all nations, I call the
naked submersion a baptism, a demonstration
that Swedenborg's visions will be a significant
resource for future poets and seers. I think of
Blake, Yeats, and indeed Malcolm Lowry, a writer
who makes the climax to his major work, *Under
the Volcano*, a plunge into the slit of a ravine
of refuse and dead dogs, a barranca. Fiction is
never quite enough. In life, echoing Swedenborg,
Lowry tumbled, drunk, into a Mexican sewage
ditch as rank as London's Gully-hole.

It has been claimed by P L Johnson, in the
newsletter of the Swedenborg Society, that the
distressed mystic never did make that messianic
fall into the filth of London: he was taking a
swim in the Fleet. The Fetter Lane lodgings are
a short stroll down Fleet Street from the now
enclosed river. The streets were themselves rivers

of nightsoil, horse droppings, seasonal mud, and all of it running towards the Thames and its fouled tributaries. Johnson says that Swedenborg had 'a particular reason to bathe in 1744 as he was aware of his spiritual call, yet at the same time felt unworthy of it'. [9] Later, the point of crisis passed, Swedenborg chose to live among the wells and bathhouses and reservoirs of Clerkenwell. He walked, so it is said, beside Hugh Myddleton's New River.

Now I'm going to talk about myths of origin. There's a book by Peter Ackroyd called *Thames: Sacred River*. Having achieved, with *London, The Biography*, an epic socio-cultural account that presents itself as a form of refracted autobiography, the autobiography of his obsessions and holy relics, Ackroyd turns his attention to the Thames. The passage between source and sea. The ribbon of dream that underwrites the materiality and realpolitik of a city founded on trade. He has always claimed that certain areas of the city have their individual sense of time. There are privileged spatial-temporal vortices in which correspondences occur. Particular qualities specific to, say, Clerkenwell or Limehouse or Southwark, come through again and again. Talking, in his biography of Blake, about the episode when William and Catherine are discovered unclothed in their Hercules Road bower, playing at Adam and Eve, Ackroyd quotes Swedenborg: 'Nakedness corresponds to innocence'. [10] He would recognize that electing to live beside Cold Bath Square, and to walk out alongside the New River, are choices that signal an affinity with ritual cleansing, drinking from source, rebirth.

We are in a haunted place tonight, echoing other talks, tapping older sources. One of the striking aspects of this area of the city—Holborn, Fleet Street, Hatton Garden, Chancery Lane—is how often, as with Swedenborg, science and industry combine with poetry. Swedenborg's New Siphon for moving water, perhaps inspired by his observation of Myddleton's canal, can be derived from the same physical territory as the garret in which the poet Chatterton kills himself. Ackroyd highlights this notion of transformation, mud to gold, gold to mud, by transferring, for a work of fiction, the alchemist John Dee's house, from Mortlake to Clerkenwell. And, in much the same fashion, Gresham College can be tracked to its original site in the City of London, and to its complicated relationship with politics and power, its pivotal role in the shift from a medieval belief system to the new sciences. The kind of world in which John Dee could be both a practising alchemist conversing with angels and an imperial geographer to the court of Elizabeth I.

I live in what was once a working-class area with an awkward, leftist council and a history of proudly independent thought; a large, sprawling, rough-edged borough called Hackney. Hackney, before the coming of the canals and railways, was quite a desirable suburb. It was a modest step outside the city walls, an area of market gardens, farms, and brick kilns. There were manor houses with orchards, an established pastoral tradition, schools for young ladies. And all these blessings derived from the existence of a founding river, the Hackney Brook. Now bricked over, made into a sewer, lost to us.

I'm going to give you a brief history of my engagement with the Hackney Brook, but I think we should first of all take the conceit of the 'lost' river as being applicable to the whole of London. How do we define a lost river? Are these simply rivers that have become degraded by exploitation, the excesses of mechanical industry? They are present, certainly, their names coded into the streets, but you'd hardly know that they're there. Or are we talking about rivers that have disappeared—been culverted— and I think that's more like it. In the mid-nineteenth century, there was a moment when many inconvenient tributaries were culverted, because we needed to introduce, by way of the civil engineer, Sir Joseph Bazalgette, a very

effective sewage system. A circuit of London's
waste to be washed away, purified, dumped in the
Thames. This was a difficult and dangerous city
in which to live; drawing water from standpipes,
from pumps in the street. There was a cholera
epidemic. It was a regular occurrence and
therefore steps had to be taken: a sewage system
was a proud Victorian boast of progress, contrived
to lift the citizens of this powerful imperial
metropolis away from the fetid stinks and oozes
of the earlier, louder and stickier city of collisions.
Regular plagues culled the legions of the massed
poor in their insanitary hovels and rookeries.
The old rivers, with their intensely local benefits
and pastoral memory traces, were also deemed
anachronistic. Either rivers were of use, for
transport or water power, or they were hidden, as
carriers of disease and conduits of filth and waste.

Probably the most mythologized of
London's lost rivers is the Fleet. We are close
to that valley now, close to the place where
Swedenborg is supposed to have plunged for

his life-transforming ritual bath. The Fleet
is a living presence for many London writers
and poets—most recently for Aidan Andrew
Dun, whose long poem, *Vale Royal*, registers
the accretions of fable associated with what he
calls the 'River of Wells'. Dun tracks the Fleet
from the seven springs of Kenwood, through
Camden Town to Kings Cross. He speaks of a
river famous 'for healing and medicinal waters'.
His lyric prospectus seems to imply, in triplets of
regular verse, that the New Jerusalem will draw
its vigour from the meaning and mythology of
the Fleet. In practical terms, he leads walks that
he calls 'river pilgrimages' through the historic
traces of the submerged stream. 'Water possessed
wisdom', he says, shepherding his troop of urban
supplicants to the Red Fountain, where they are
invited 'to taste the holy waters', before moving
on to the tumulus of Boudicca. *Vale Royal* gives
prominence to an episode when Chatterton is
supposed to have tumbled into an open grave
in St Pancras Churchyard, close to the Fleet;

another version perhaps of the mud baptism.
'The days of the superterranean man are over!'[11]

    The Fleet, flowing down the valley right behind
us, has a close relationship with Smithfield
Market: it's thickened and clogged by morbidity,
the butchery of animals and the disposal of
hoofs, horns, carcasses, dogs, rats, birds. Gutters
thick with blood and fat. A river polluted by the
slaughter of living creatures becomes, perversely,
one of the energizing zones of a city. A zone with
narrow streets still holding to their Elizabethan
proportions. Open spaces in which religious
martyrs, proud heretics, were barbecued. A zone
with memories of the circle of alchemists around
David Dee, Rector of St Bartholomew's Church,
and kinsman to the magus, Dr John Dee. Cities
self-assemble around their essential markets—
meat, fish, vegetables, the clothes and effects of
the dead—before those markets are expelled, for
reasons of convenience, to the suburbs; in the
same way that asylums and hospitals are often
pushed out from the centre, hidden at the limits

of visibility, to mark the boundary between city and country. Psychosis and breakdown belong to the areas where humans are most closely packed together; our instinct, Foucault teaches us, is to push disease away, to isolate it, to avoid contamination. Dis-ease: that which is alien, that which makes us uncomfortable.

Billingsgate Fish Market, once a true watergate, marking riverside entrance to Trinovantum, and dedicated to the legendary king Belinus, was uprooted and transported to Docklands, as a spectacle to be noticed on the Docklands Light Railway. Spitalfields Market has relocated to Stratford and the Olympic Park. The established routes for travelling through the labyrinth of a city towards an old market become liberties, special forms of permission, routes down which you're allowed to move your cattle or flocks from green spaces like London Fields in Hackney, where animals are fattened on good grass, or where geese recover after a squawking march from Norfolk. Those streets are chartered, they acquire particular enterprises, public houses, brothels, small traders looking to supply the drovers. What does Blake say in his poem, 'London'?

I wander thro' each charter'd street, / Near where the charter'd Thames does flow / And mark in every face I meet / Marks of weakness, marks of woe. [12]

The Fleet, at first such a small secret, comes to us from the heights of Hampstead, where you overlook the spread of the city. There are memories of Constable's cloud paintings; you have *space*, the city as an event horizon, a subject for contemplation. The Fleet is just one thread, leading you past St Pancras Old Church, which Aidan Dun calls the 'keystone' of *Vale Royal*. The church was built no later than 312 AD and is therefore, Dun asserts, linked 'with the first centuries of the Christian age in Britain, the period of Constantine the Great and his

mother St Helena, the time of The Grail Cycle
legends, even with the time of Christ's actual
visit to Britain'. On its raised island of turf, the
church is shipwrecked by all the developments
around Kings Cross. There are so many local
associations: with the poet Shelley who met Mary
Shelley among the graves, with Chatterton, with
Rimbaud who lodged in Royal College Street
with his bedfellow, Verlaine—and with Thomas
Hardy as an apprentice architect who, when the
railways were carving through the graveyard, got
the job of tidying away the stones. They cluster
around the tree that carries his name like sharks'
fins: another watery metaphor from the floating
city. Another reminder of days that have been, or
days to come, when the seas roll over all these
vain stones.

London's rivers have a dark side too. There are
as many suicides as baptisms. That impulse, the
muddy plunge, the rebirth, remains a constant.
The photographer Stephen Gill, wandering the
Lower Lea Valley, the reed beds and murky side

channels, came across one such ceremony:
a charismatic black preacher in a white suit
dipping members of his congregation into the
industrial river.

As Joseph Conrad knew, better than anyone,
better even than Eliot, one river is all rivers.
'Forthwith a change came over the waters, and
the serenity became less brilliant but more
profound', he wrote in the sonorous opening
movement of *Heart of Darkness*. [13] There was
a moment when Christopher Wren felt that
he could initiate, with a revamp of the Fleet, a
new Venice, right at the river's mouth, close to
St Paul's Cathedral: a shining rational city of
domes and bridges and splendid public works.

More recently planners and promoters have
had the same fantasy for the Lower Lea: a park
of commerce and leisure and inward investment.
Constructed around a new cathedral, the
Westfield supermall. Rivers and railways, those
glistening rivers of steel. Agents of progress.
Agents of destruction. Wren didn't have CGI

futurism as a tool, ersatz utopianism, but he did
have drawings that suggested Fleet-as-Venice
would become a wonder of the age. Except
that, very soon, and inevitably, the river was a
ditch, a sewage creek crusted with dead dogs.
Street children, drunks, and even perhaps the
occasional mystic, swam there, until the river
was enclosed, sealed over, lost. Until, centuries
later, in the late 1940s, you arrive at the point
where Carol Reed is making his famous film
The Third Man in Vienna, and there's a pursuit,
Orson Welles in flapping overcoat running
through picturesque sewers. Welles was not very
keen on going down into the tunnels, so they
ended up recording sound effects under London:
in the Fleet. This is such an adaptable space, a
space caught up with its own mythology. But that
sweep of sound, the rush of floodwater, is heard
only by those professional subterraneans, the
sewermen. Or by researchers, steeling themselves
to confront the worst, in quest of a better story.
Rachel Lichtenstein, towards the close of

Diamond Street: The Hidden World of Hatton Garden, dons hard-hat, wellington boots and protective suit, to make the plunge.

> *We stood for some time in the water of the vast chamber, the most dreamlike space I have ever encountered, admiring the incredibly beautiful brickwork, listening to the sound of the rushing water, the clanking of the giant flaps behind us gently swaying as the river rushed past...*
>
> *We were physically underneath the city but had entered a different realm, there was nothing in that space apart from ourselves to suggest we were in the twenty-first century. I had managed to achieve something, if only for a few brief moments, which I had been trying to do since I started this project: to peel back the veil of time, to glimpse a moment of the past, to walk in a landscape from a bygone era.* [14]

Blake, talking about secret rivers in *Jerusalem*, says:

> *The banks of the Thames are clouded! The*
> *ancient porches of Albion are / Darken'd!*
> *they are drawn thro' unbounded space,*
> *scatter'd upon / The Void in incoherent*
> *despair!*

And again:

> *From Highgate's heights and Hampstead's*
> *to Poplar, Hackney and Bow; / To Islington*
> *and Paddington and the brook of Albion's*
> *river, / We builded Jerusalem as a city and*
> *as a temple.* [15]

Hidden rivers are part of an attempt to found
a celestial city above the degraded particulars
of the nexus of business and banking. The
champagne bars and lap-dancing pits. Aidan
Dun references what he calls the 'Golden
Quatrain' of Blake; pillars of gold set down in

Islington, Marylebone, Primrose Hill, St John's
Wood. There is also the unregistered darkness
of water beneath the ground. The rivers that
we sense but no longer see. In the *Notes* that
accompany the poem of *Vale Royal*, Dun says:
'The black stream is a ley-line whose energies
have become stagnant through neglect,
or negative through misuse'. Two kinds of
water are always present. Or indeed a single
mysterious substance capable of those shifts
and metamorphoses Conrad noticed, from
shimmering sundance tesserae to occulted black
in an instant: 'less brilliant but more profound'.

At one time in my random and unfocused career,
in the early 1970s or late '60s, I was working as
a painter and decorator at a flat in Chepstow
Place in Notting Hill——and was interested to
discover that 16 Chepstow Place was the address
of a certain Mr Malthus, a member of the Suicide
Club in Robert Louis Stevenson's *New Arabian
Nights.* I was very keen on Stevenson, and much

taken with the coincidences and overlaps that
are part of any life in a big city. This was a
house with atmosphere. Pre-fictional. Possessed.
Most of the daylight hours we were scraping
at the walls, in the dust, making preparations
for the moment when the paint would be
applied. I'm not sure that we ever reached it.
Around one o'clock, or more probably *exactly*
at one o'clock, every day, I heard this strange
tapping sound—*puck plup puck plub*—from
somewhere outside, but close. Or was it in the
wall? Like moths headbutting a lightbulb. Or
some newly solidified liquid dripping on a
Formica surface. And then I realized, looking
out of the window, that the sound came from two
people, down below in an enclosed courtyard,
wearing mufflers, wooly hats, long coats, gloves
and dark glasses, playing an intensely serious,
silent, monkish game of table tennis. It was very
Cartesian, dignified and absurd. I thought at
once of Beckett. Later on, asking our employer
about this scene, I learnt the identities of the

combatants: Donald McWhinnie and his wife. McWhinnie was the producer of several Beckett plays for the BBC's Third Service. After twenty minutes, precisely, they stopped, whatever the state of play, and they retreated back inside like figures on a cuckoo clock.

I was brooding on the weirdness of this part of town, Wyndham Lewis's *Rotting Hill*, as I walked back to the tube station——where I was confronted by banner headlines about a savage murder that had occurred in a neighbouring street. This was James Pope-Hennessy, the well-connected biographer, who was also known as a serious drinker and familiar of afternoon clubs and cellars. The unfinished biography on his desk, when he was beaten to death by a casual pick-up, was of Stevenson. It was published posthumously without revision. In 1945 he shared a flat with Guy Burgess. Coincidences, overlaps, connections. Pope-Hennessy's first book, which won the Hawthornden Prize in 1939, was called *London Fabric*.

The Chepstow Place house seemed to float on a reservoir of dark waters. Julian Maclaren-Ross, the great flâneur and confabulator, roosted in the same Suicide Club flat, as he worked on his final book. The game was up. He was overprepared for his afterlife in Soho memoirs and the novels of Anthony Powell. Stevenson, Maclaren-Ross, Beckett. Scratching at layers of old paint was like revealing a memory-chapel of all the buried rivers. The only sound, until the one o'clock table tennis—even when it was muffled by snowfall—was of the scraper working its way across the white autopsy screen of the wall. Waiting for the words to bleed through.

And here is where the merely uncanny dissolves into a paranoid super-critical mass worthy of Philip K Dick or David Lynch. Maclaren-Ross, with his saturation in alcohol and lost literature, gothic and pulp, assigns his moral collapse to Stevenson. In a very useful biography, *Fear and Loathing in Fitzrovia: The Strange Lives of Julian Maclaren-Ross*,

Paul Willetts explains. 'By then homeless and so mentally unbalanced that he became convinced his personality had been taken over by the villain from Robert Louis Stevenson's *Dr Jekyll and Mr Hyde*, he sold the pristine manuscript to raise money.' Text, under the influence of buried rivers, becomes porous. Dr Jekyll's house is the model of a skull split between starchy respectability and a private laboratory where a second, bestial self can be readied for engagement with the night streets. The dandified author-actor, Maclaren-Ross, fixing his own legend, picks his final address with forensic exactitude. He knew just what he was doing, and where he had to be. 'By 1951', Willetts wrote, 'financial necessity had compelled him to accept more screenwriting work, this time providing an updated, never-to-be-produced adaptation of Robert Louis Stevenson's *The Suicide Club*'. [16]

Our Chepstow Place employer, Carol Williams, lived here as a child. The house had been designed by her architect father, it meant a lot

to her. She wrote a fine piece recalling those
early days for a book I edited, *London, City of
Disappearances*. Her mother, a young Jewish
girl escaping from Innsbruck, just in time,
underwent a 'terrifying search' at the Italian
border. 'Among the items returned to her, as she
got back on the train, was the single book she'd
brought, to practice English on the journey:
Stevenson's *New Arabian Nights*.' Carol's
parents met, so she tells us, 'playing table tennis
in a village by an Austrian lake.' But the most
haunting recollection, never quite brought into
focus, was of 'a river under the garden'. Perhaps
it had been a dream? An elderly neighbour,
interrogated, confirmed the suspicion. There
was a buried river, it had affected the building
work. 'Bad drainage is the least of what you get
when you build between streams (Coulters Creek,
Westbourne River),' Carol wrote. 'It takes huge
imagination to match above what lies below.
When that fails, danger and stagnation follow.'
The house of Carol's childhood was number

32—but her mother, in what proved a precarious investment, later acquired number 16: the house of Stevenson's Suicide Club and the last days of Maclaren-Ross. The house of table tennis rituals. And the flat I had been asked to decorate. 'The address', Carol concludes, 'is a dark fiction.' [17]

A dowser I spoke to, as he confirmed the hidden route of the Hackney Brook, from the River Lea to its source alongside Holloway Road, produced a device for measuring the risks we face from unseen rivers. I had invited the dowser to join me on my journey in order to make sure I was going the right way, staying close to the lost river. He was a man who had been made redundant by the Ford factory in Dagenham and who had taken up dowsing as his second career. He said, 'There is a disease pattern in certain districts of London, malfunction, malfate. I have researched those patterns, followed the viral rings outwards, like the ripples from a stone dropped in a pond. Houses built above lost rivers, if the inhabitants have no knowledge of that history, carry a dark

aura. Ill fortunate is always associated with this.
Look, I have a disk with which I can measure the
effect. Watch the pendulum'.

Aidan Dun reminds us that the Fleet 'still runs
under Kings Cross today'. To provide the motor
for his poem. 'As late as the mid-nineteenth
century', he says, 'it ran on the surface through a
green and pleasant land. But south of the Euston
Road at this period it was already bricked-over
and buried'. So he dedicates *Vale Royal* to
the zone around Kings Cross and St Pancras
Old Church. And by an act of extreme self-
hypnosis, he becomes convinced that the present
developments, that narcissism of dark glass,
the glittering arts centres, the forced gardens,
newspaper offices, riverside apartments, are
somehow a manifestation of Blake's vision, or an
extension of Swedenborg's multiple city: the New
Jerusalem. To return the favour, the promoters of
this territory emblazon a triad from Dun's poem,
The Brill, on a wall in Granary Square (where no
water mills grind bread).

*Kings Cross, dense with angels and
histories / there are cities beneath your
pavements / cities behind your skies. Let
me see!* [18]

Dun's spiritual copywriting, intended for a pot
of paint and a railway arch, is now sited, loud
and bright, at the centre of the development. And
what he is reasserting is the Swedenborgian logic
of the London of lost rivers. 'Cities beneath the
pavements.' Enlightenment in the Gully-hole.
'They rejoiced that now as before they are in
England, and in its great city,' Swedenborg wrote
in *The Last Judgment*. 'And they said that there
is also another London below, not dissimilar as
to the streets.' [19] A city of sleepwalkers, soft at its
core, sinking into the hellish depths.

Vale Royal is both post-Swedenborgian and
pre-Swedenborgian; innocent, canny, open to
echoes, and closed in on itself like a coffin made
from mirrors. Swedenborg dreams of a city of the
living dead with its centre close to Holborn, to the

hall where we find ourselves tonight. Dun sees his task as the revelation of the theology of a hidden river, the Fleet. He attempts—and there is hubris in this—the restoration of a sacred dimension, by way of the rhythms and repetitions of his post-druidic triads. He wants to trace a particular thread, as the river curves around the island of the old church, a building dressed with engravings of boys swimming in a living stream, swimming to heaven. Are they reaching towards the skies or sinking beneath cloud-reflecting waters?

The stream rushes on, now under the pavements, slaughterhouses, prisons, book stalls, down the valley of the Fleet, towards myths of albino hogs in the sludge of dripping subterranean spaces. There's a book called *Black Swine in the Sewers of Hampstead (Beneath the Surface of Victorian Sensationalism)* by Thomas Boyle. Legends of animals, escaped from Smithfield, feeding on refuse, living in darkness. Boyle quotes *The Daily Telegraph* of October 10, 1859. 'This London is an amalgam of worlds

within worlds . . . It has been said that . . .
Hampstead sewers shelter a monstrous breed of
black swine, which have propagated and run wild
among the slimy feculence, and whose ferocious
snouts will one day up-root Highgate archway,
while making Holloway intolerable with their
grunting.' Boyle connects these lurid fables with a
metropolitan sense of 'decomposing symmetry'.[20]
With a pre-Freudian vision of the 'seething
cauldron' of the subconscious. And later, we
recall, Freud settles with his family in Hampstead,
on the hill under which the new railways bore
and burrow. Cabinets are filled with fetishes and
Egyptian votive figures, beast-gods obsessively
collected, arranged like a map of the mind.

Dun takes it further. He tracks the Fleet under
Farringdon and down to the Thames. In Holborn,
the buried river facilitates a miasma of disease,
cholera, typhoid; a conduit of mephitic air,
bubbling green slime, carcasses and anatomical
leftovers from Bart's Hospital suppurating
against the barrier of the watergate. A poem,

conservative in diction, and in its spiritual and psychic address, acknowledges London's plural nature: city within city, upside-down topography, rivers flowing under the ground, heaven inside the ball of earth.

By way of contrast, I would look at the way two late-modernist London poets, Bill Griffiths and Allen Fisher, treat our lost rivers. Both of them track South London streams, in the thick of local particulars, towards an erased history, to emerge in the contemporary world of political opportunism, civic discord. Open-field poetics against Dun's formal triads. The recovered rivers of Griffiths and Fisher spurt and slop and vanish. They make a map of the page of text. They do not fold back into the rictus of orthodox derangement. These quests are modest and unresolved.

after the Sluice walked upstream / along a connecting stream to Neckinger / (the course between Bermondsey Abbey & Thames) / parts of the flow are artificial...

took the bus south / I couldn't get to the
matter of this / if our streams are becoming
artificial / our old sources will die [21]

Fisher keeps a record, a fragmented diary of
his expeditions, in the books gathered as *Place*.
It is hard to imagine the elevated Dun reporting
from a bus. He seems to float, long scarf flying, a
few inches from the ground. Bill Griffiths, Celtic
scholar, former Hell's Angel, tramps the Wandle to
its dissolution under the car park of a multistore.

As to the past, dig up, gone, went, start
now, economically. / Rumours. Druids.
The round bit. I like that, / Zod this. Here
store. Here carpark. Here muddy hole. In /
middle. Mad. [22]

From such a distinctive angle of approach,
predatory, circling the subject, beating to a wilder
drum, Griffiths arrives at the same metaphor for
transcendence: the muddy hole. Under tarmac,

under the ranks of suburban shoppers: madness. Mud baptism.

Fisher returns the story to Charles Olson, whose methods he adapts to Brixton. You find out everything there is about your place. And then you must lift beyond it. The first movement of Fisher's *Place* is about fixing the chart, feeling his way along those lost rivers.

> *if I take a river to its source / and in the case of the Falcon Brook / this is 2 springs / & follow its course / from head to tail / to the Thames / I may arrive from at least three projections / the source in the springs / is not the actual source / but the first visible source / so that if Pound said it / it is original / this originality has come because of previous accumulation*

However contradictory your approach to writing about the city, whether you're a modernist using conceptual methods of research, combined with walking, bus trips, photography, painting, or whether you're a traditional poet obedient to strict form, rivers infiltrate your projections as memory strips or teasing songlines. 'The course becomes the sewer / where our roots suck for vertu', Fisher says.[23]

When I began my project of writing a kind of mnemonic, personal history, local history of my native borough, the book that became *Hackney, That Rose-Red Empire*, I felt that there were a lot of negative energies in play. I could see the areas that I would be satirical about. I could see hideous building schemes imposed under the rubric of Olympic legacy. I could register the manifold disappearances. But where were the positives? What would change when the dust settled? It was an engraving of the vanished Hackney Brook that proved the inspiration for another way of looking at the future. The river had been covered over in 1861, but it was still very much a presence. If you encountered engravings of St Augustine's Church at the top end of Mare Street, the atmosphere was bucolic. The river crossed the road in front of the church. There was a footbridge. A set of historic images, now frequently degraded, photocopied, bleached out, surfaced as hard evidence of something lost. They would be pasted on walls as a riposte to the amnesia of the present moment. The Hackney Brook doesn't flow into the Thames, it flows into the River Lea, right alongside the point where the Northern Sewage Outfall is pumped through elevated pipes. The Brook rises beside Holloway Road, close to the foothills of Highgate. There are two springs. When the waters are conjoined, they sweep around Highbury, the old Arsenal Stadium; then through the northern edge of Abney Park Cemetery; across Sandy Ford, at the bottom of Stamford Hill, and under Hackney Downs on the west side. Mare Street into Morning Lane. And, finally, into the Lea beyond Old Ford Lock. Well Street causes frequent problems for Thames Water operatives, burst pipes and the like. When I was walking with the dowser, we met folk in Stoke Newington, across the road from Abney

Park, who told us that their cellars tended to flood whenever there was a heavy storm. They blamed it on the lost river.

The Brook is there and, buried or not, it defines the area. You appreciate the reason for the siting of the grander houses, the lost villas and formal gardens on the ridge above Morning Lane. You register, despite everything, the hysteria of development, the mess of declining industries, the geological soul of the place. With water as the transmitter. History can be recovered, through careful observation, keeping your ear to the ground. Sutton House is visible evidence. You can step inside, tap the walls, experience the chain of evidence that accompanies you on any journey from spring to source. The river is the reason that this place grows up. There are no disappearances, only reappearances, as we enjoy sudden flares of consciousness and recognition.

Walking around the fringes of London, I began to think that the true river for contemporary London

was not the Thames but the orbital motorway,
the M25. It carried the goods and traffic of the
world. It hummed and throbbed with a babble
of electronic chatter. And it went nowhere. It
was entirely self-referential, letting you off into
aborted versions of the past, of nineteenth-century
science fiction: Dracula's abbey at Purfleet, the
Martian invaders of H G Wells stomping across
the river at Shepperton. Not being permitted, as
an unvehicled pedestrian, to walk over the QEII
bridge at Dartford, from Kent to Essex, means a
long detour to catch the ferry at Gravesend. Which
brings you up against the opening of Joseph
Conrad's *Heart of Darkness*; being held on the
tide, the wealth of London as a trading port on
the western horizon, all the great rivers waiting.
London was enriched by these connections: India,
the Indies, China. Well, that wasn't happening
anymore, the Thames had ceased to be a viable
port with deepwater docks, busy quays. It was a
strip of heritage, vainglorious interventions, to be
fought over and decorated with Ferris wheels and

necklaces of airline-sponsored ski lifts. The M25
motorway, the tarmac tourniquet, its grey glitter
mistaken for water by incoming swans, was the
functioning link with global enterprise. It had
the cargoes of Europe and the Orient, legitimate
and illegitimate. Service stations were like docks,
like the old Ratcliffe Highway: time out, rest and
recreation, provisions, beds, booze. The trading
stations Conrad experienced along the malarial
Congo were absorbed into the retail-park swamps
of the A13: the smoking landfill ridges, the oil
refineries, the new (and already half-abandoned)
estates on the flood plain of Thames Gateway. The
M25 is a visible river, a river in a bright yellow
hi-viz jacket, but its soul and spirit are constantly
challenged. The subterranean rivers, the invisible
rivers so many people are keen on recovering,
continue as a secret history. I wanted to align
myself with that version of the story.

I went to Old Ford Lock, not far from where
the Hackney Brook trickles into the River Lea.
It's the point where a back channel detours

into the Olympic Park. When the blue fence
went up, entirely enclosing the old orchards
and allotments of the Park, the only access was
by water. With Stephen Gill, and later with the
painter Jock McFadyen, using an inflatable
kayak, we managed to navigate, as if going on
some crazy Herzog voyage over the rapids at the
head waters of the Amazon, through this hidden
landscape, where there was dense vegetation,
kingfishers flashing blue, derelict squats and
warehouses. It was absolutely magical. Our
expeditions carried on for maybe a month or so
until I made the mistake of talking about it on
the radio. The next time we went down there, a
big chain with yellow spikes had been set across
the channel as an impenetrable barrier.

I tried to write about my sense of a terrain in
transition, an edgeland of lost rivers about to be
re-exploited, reverse engineered, obliterated.

*Old Ford, out of Fish Island, was a num-
inous locale in London's deep-topography:*

the crossing place on the River Lea—which was once a major obstacle, a much broader stream. Here was a border between cultures, between Vikings and Saxons, pagans and Christians, travellers and fixed citizens, the living and the dead.

The critic John Adlard, back in 1973, had the interesting idea that William Blake confused Old Ford with Stratford. In a short essay, he wrote of Blake walking, in a single day, 'up to forty miles in the environs of London'. But Jerusalem *is not the record of a gruelling hike, it is the heartbeat of a 'mental traveller'. Los, Blake's solar daemon, blazes like a comet. He maps energies, not in the robotic voice of a Sat Nav system, but with rhythms of blood; pulsing, hammering, driven onwards.*

What Adlard struggles with is a topography that detours east to Stratford, before heading down to the Isle of Dogs. It strikes me that Los is not following the

*money but predicting its swinish rush on
unexploited brownfield sites: Docklands
and the future Stratford City, with its
Olympic rings and satellite parks. 'All the
tendernesses of the soul cast forth as filth
& mire.'*

*This is a vision without boundaries.
Outside time. And not, certainly not,
the limited prospect of pre-Olympic mud
offered to the privileged few from Holden
Point, the twenty-one-storey Stratford tower
block, where a fit and vulpine Lord Coe
throws back the silken linings of his deep-
blue jacket, like a fallen angel, to offer the
kingdoms of the virtual world, its mounds
and stadia, to investors prepared to
mortgage a city's future on the demolition
and ransacking of a mythical past.* [24]

As preparation, this morning, for thinking
about rivers, secret or otherwise, I re-walked the
Blakean route back to Stratford Olympic Park

and I noticed, or re-noticed, something I hadn't seen for a long time. As you come out of Victoria Park, going towards the car park and Wick Lane, towards a pub called *Top o' the Morning*, which is so stridently Celtic it doesn't really need the two Irish flags to make the point, there's a wall, a low brick wall draped by overhanging greenery. It has been there, I guess, for thirty or more years, and it depicts one of the lost rivers of London: the pastoral Lea of Izaak Walton. Of course the Lea is still there, but it's not the same river. The narrowboats are under sufferance, threatened by waterside development, and newcomers complaining about smoke and noise.

The modest and peeling mural in Victoria Park represents Hackney as an arcadia for knapsacked ramblers, fishermen. It is touching to find this aspirational fantasy, signed by a cluster of the local people who produced it, confronting the Greenway (or former Sewage Outfall), where the Olympic exclusion zone begins. The air hums and buzzes until your ears

ring; cranes sway, you taste the red dust. And still
the mural survives, this vision of hybrid London,
rus in urbe, snaking away to source, beyond
the reservoirs, parks, spring pools. There are no
people, it's rather like Blake: 'human form is
none'. And, because there are no people, there is
no fixed sense of time. The Lower Lea Valley is
both timeless and permanent, and the only thing
that's happening is the cheap paint is coming
away, bright orange red bricks showing through,
absorbing the small history of water.

When, rather reluctantly, you let the frozen
cinema of this river-based propaganda go, and
you step away, and you pass on towards the
canal, the man-made speculations, there is a
very dramatic change in imagery. A rush of the
new: like a compulsory chemical hit, a forced
prescription. Liquid cosh. This is public energy,
loud, blatant, and above all *accountable*. Walls
and fences are dense with CGI futurism. Realities
that don't exist now in any other form and which
will never exist. Here is that painted park wall

with a billion-pound budget: gleaming stadia of corporate endorsements and hyper-convincing leisure facilities, many of which have already been downsized or cancelled.

Away from the art of unreality, and not yet expelled, are burrows of Hackney Wick community artists, endgame guerillas. The river brought them here. And the river is their battleground. They respond to the digital propaganda with spray cans and stencils. They work with a neurotic intensity, mile after mile splashed with a sticky bestiary of apocalypse. The cartoon violence invokes the Mexican muralists, children of surrealism and revolution. There are mangled Mayan and Aztec quotations, a lot of serpents and snakes and gashed mouths and bleeding eyes. By night, the artists crawl over buildings that are about to be demolished, releasing giant crocodiles and monster rats to slide back into the Mesozoic swamp like lost paragraphs of early Ballard. The demented productivity of the anti-pantheon, the compulsive post-industrial noise of the unlicensed

and unapproved, animates the back channels
and polluted rivers. Bridges, warehouses, wharfs:
they have replaced the railways as suitable
territory for Blakean signatures, the banners for
a doctrine of expulsion and disenfranchisement.

It was tough to record these manifestations.
Gash muralists were ambitious of becoming
the next Banksy. Digital transfers were made
as soon as the latest outrage was perpetrated.
Everything, all new energies, can be exploited.
Content is devoured like candyfloss. The Mayans,
apparently, see August 2012 as the end of a
five-thousand-year cycle. The winged serpent of
time is already in the skies over Stratford like
one of the new camera drones bought in from
Afghanistan. There are five suns symbolized
by the five Olympic rings. Ever more fantastic
temples are required, that stacked box-cathedral
of the Westfield Supermall was inevitable.
Worshippers are lining up from deep Essex,
Hackney and Thames Gateway, even if they can't
afford to actually shop. Under surveillance,

they process through the courts and corridors,
waiting to sip the sacred coffee-bean essence.
Waterfalls tumble from high-definition screens,
but you can't drink them. And you don't get wet.
Westfield has abolished weather. The only thing
underneath this monolith is a car park.

I went this morning to see the place where
I'd worked as a labourer when I first came to
Hackney. It was called Chobham Farm, and
sounded absolutely delightful, but was set down
among the railway sheds of Stratford. You
unloaded containers and stacked the contents,
before shifting them to vans and lorries: inland
dockwork to circumvent the stranglehold of the
unions. A cowboy operation as forerunner of
much grander piracies to come. The cargoes of
the world again: fruit, wine, spanners, household
effects, talcum powder, the reek and drip of sheep
casings. The promoters felt that the rivers were
dying, the Thames was no longer a working river
and the dockers were an ugly anachronism of
restrictive practices. When rivers lose their status,

spiritually and materially, the land is drained of value. First the monasteries disappeared and then the factories of the second industrial revolution.

One afternoon a consignment of beautiful Italian washing machines arrived and we were issued with sledgehammers and told to smash them, because the purchaser wanted to claim insurance. 'Trash the lot', they said, 'then mark the forms with "damaged in transit", a storm at sea'. I remember the Stratford landscape as a desert of earth mounds and naked mud, huge hoists and railway lines replacing the slow and steady barge traffic of the canals and inland navigation systems. What has emerged, with Westfield, the transport hub, the Olympics, is anti-river, anti-flow; a CGI denial of the freedom to drift and wander; a reflex suspension of permissions, cancelled footpaths, chained rivers. It was my instinct to oppose these gigantic enclosures by walking beside water, swimming to heaven, making a respectful march along the traces of the buried Hackney Brook in company with a dowser. I think of the company of Londoners who drew sustenance from the mystique of this water margin: coracle makers, fishermen, gardeners, naturalists, oarsmen (and women), cyclists. Along with painters and photographers like Stephen Gill, Jock McFadyen, Mimi Mollica, Emily Richardson, Laura Oldfield Ford.

This walk was my equivalent of Swedenborg's mud baptism, or Blake's vision in Peckham: 'a tree filled with angels, bright angelic wings bespangling every bough like stars'. The walk was necessary and specific, and the interesting thing was, having done it once by myself, to confirm the shape, the rewiring of brain chemistry, by doing it again with the dowser. He confirmed the starting point beside the Lea and then we curled around Victoria Park. You could feel the power of the lost river, right alongside the road where we were walking. Climbing a fence, we found a rather inviting patch of wild wood in the shadow of the Eastway. It was not easily accessible, which made it all the more attractive.

An invisible community, a tribe leaving signs of a recent campsite behind them, were living under the motorway. They had decorated the concrete with drawings and cuttings from magazines. They left sleeping bags and books swollen with rainwater and blackened by smoke. It was as if they had chosen to cluster around the memory of the Hackney Brook. I thought again of anthropologists and explorers pushing down the Amazon, hacking through jungles, finding deserted settlements.

But time is pressing, and we've put out a long way from shore, so I'll finish with an element from this river walk. As we came down Morning Lane, we ran up against the usual Hackney excavations, workmen standing around a hole in the road. They told us that every time they started to dig, the hole flooded before they could repair the old Victorian water pipes. This was all the confirmation we needed: that we were still on the track of the Hackney Brook, as it curved through the valley of formerly grand houses, past the watercress beds, now colonized by Tesco. In fact, the latest civic scheme is to make Tesco a primary agent of regeneration, to surround the supermarket with tower blocks; so that Hackney, the riverside village, becomes a suburb of Tesco, rather than the other way round.

As the day progressed and as we dropped deeper into the songline of the Brook, our river walk became intertwined with another notion, the Northwest Passage. This goes back, in my London mythology, all the way to Thomas De Quincey and *The Confessions of an English Opium-Eater*. De Quincey describes how he is absorbed and cobwebbed into the dense gravity of the centre of London and how he attempts, in panicked rushes and starts, to navigate a path out of the labyrinth by way of close passages, alleyways, secret courtyards. The ritual can still be experienced in Bishopsgate, the City, Clerkenwell, Holborn. You progress like a stream of water, running up against barriers and blockages, detouring, doubling back. You're flung out onto the street, you duck and dive. Inspired by the early voyagers and venturers, Sir Hugh Willoughby, Sir Martin Frobisher, and their search for the 'Arctic Grail', De Quincey contemplated a hidden path out of London, his own Northwest Passage. He would stumble across a particular street that led into another street. He would lose himself, trust in blind instinct. Walk by night. He would move through other dimensions.

His concept was picked up by later authors like Arthur Machen, who decided that the promising area to explore was suburban Hackney, Stoke Newington. Which brings us back, very neatly, to the Hackney Brook. And my feeling that we were escaping from the monolithic density of the new by tracking an old river. I'll read you an extract from *Hackney, That Rose-Red Empire* dealing with the Stoke Newington passage of our walk.

Hacking into tangled undergrowth, as clinging, dense and light-devouring as my book had become, bumping against

obscured gravestones and the sharp wings
of ivy-cloaked angels, I remembered what
Poe and Arthur Machen had drawn from
this area: confusion, doubled identities, a
shift in the electromagnetic field. There was
a long tradition beginning with De Quincey
of searching for a Northwest Passage
out of London, away from the restrictive
conventions of time and space. The route
these men hinted at seemed to have an
intimate relation with the course of the
submerged Hackney Brook: Abney Park,
Clissold Park, pubs named after Robinson
Crusoe, the slopes of Highgate Hill.

Machen called this part of London a
'Terra Incognita'. He spoke of 'obscure
alleyways with discreet, mysterious postern
doors . . . a region beyond Ultima Thule'.
There is always a Machen theme, an
excuse to draw the unwary in. A search
for Edgar Allen Poe's school: the one he
actually attended or the more engrossing

fiction from his 'William Wilson' tale.
Autobiography mulches down to let richer
weeds break surface. Those who embark on
a London quest begin in a pub. They yarn,
they misquote, improvise. They walk out,
eventually, through a one-off topography
they are obliged to shape into a serviceable
narrative. Language creaks. 'The dreamy
village, the misty trees, the old rambling
redbrick houses, standing in their gardens,
with the high walls about them.'

There's a magic place, close to Abney
Park, that nobody can find twice. Believing
this consoling fable, I suppose, makes Stoke
Newington possible: the self-confident
self-contained inhabitants, their nice shops,
their historic library and surveillance
monitors. Living here allows you to peruse
the dangerously vulgar streets of Lesser
Hackney and to congratulate yourself
on your good fortune. Villas of successful
Nonconformist tradesmen survive. Defoe

*plaques and pubs. We enter the library
and ask to be pointed in the direction of the
local history shelves.*

*'There is no local history any more,' says
the woman at the desk. 'It's out of date.'*

*All that's been left has been relegated to
a cardboard box kept under the counter.
I buy a booklet on Clissold Park that
characteristically boasts of a connection
with William Wilberforce and the Stoke
Newington Abolitionists, while turning
a blind eye to fortunes built on the
dark trade, sugar and slavery. There is
a smudged photograph of a policeman
feeding swans on a secret river.* [25]

I come back at the end to Emanuel
Swedenborg, naked, rolling in mud, distributing
his money to the watching mob. And to the
Swedish prophet's abiding belief in the plurality
of London, his adopted city; a place where
hard science was in constant argument with

mysticism. 'There is also another London below', he says. And the centre, the point of access, is close to Holborn. According to Lars Bergquist, in *Swedenborg's Secret: A Biography*, the troubled and exhausted seer, at his time of crisis in 1744, exploited the hypnagogic state, that sense of swimming to heaven, somewhere between sleep and wakefulness. Water was the hinge. The way out from a material city of convulsive intoxication: claret, ale, laudanum for high and low, court, judiciary, mob. City of sediment whose vaults and towers of vanity are stacked beside a great river, anchored by submerged streams: Walbrook, Westbourne, Effra.

Blake saw the power of naming rivers as the naming of the gods. 'One tiny tributary of the Thames was Tyburn Brook, which passed the gallows before plunging underground', S Foster Damon tells us in *A Blake Dictionary*.

Loud sounds the Hammer of Los & loud his Bellows is heard / Before London

to Hampstead's breadths & Highgate's
heights, To / Stratford & old Bow &
across to the Gardens of Kensington / On
Tyburn's Brook: loud groans Thames
beneath the iron Forge [26]

Bill Giffiths and Allen Fisher also weave water
names into their open-field texts. The Olsonian
cover of Fisher's collected *Place*, published by
Reality Street Editions in 2005, is a map of
London hinged by the blue-grey Thames, with
Neckinger, Effra and Walbrook clearly marked
and named. The lost rivers are returned to the
surface of the city. Fisher's textual London is
'bounded by Stamford Brook & River Lea'.
Situationism cohabits with dowsers and ramblers,
bus passes to paradise.

   Aidan Dun sees the Fleet as a liquid wand
for the re-enchantment of Kings Cross. Julian
Maclaren-Ross and Robert Louis Stevenson
identify the darker, Manichean aspect of
subterranean streams brooding beneath

speculative developments in the new suburbs of the west. John Keats, born at Moorgate, dies in Rome, and chooses for his epitaph: 'Here lies One Whose Name was writ in Water'.

Thank you.

Endnotes

1   Charles Olson, *The Maximus Poems*, ed. George F Butter-
     ick (Berkeley and London: University of California Press,
     1983).
2   J H Prynne, *On Maximus IV. V. VI.* A lecture given at
     Simon Fraser University, 27 July 1971.
3   *Hackney, That Rose-Red Empire* (London: Hamish
     Hamilton, 2009).
4   Herman Melville, *Moby-Dick; or, The Whale* (New York:
     Harper & Brothers, London: Richard Bentley, 1851).
5   William Blake, *Milton*, plate 22, l. 50.
6   William Blake, *Jerusalem, The Emanation of The Giant
     Albion* (1804-20), plate 21, l. 33.
7   Charles Dickens, *Our Mutual Friend* (London: Chap-
     man & Hall, 1864-5).
8   Lars Bergquist, *Swedenborg's Dream Diary*, tr. Anders
     Hallengren (West Chester: Swedenborg Foundation, 2001).
9   P L Johnson, 'Swedenborg Not So Crazy', in *Things Heard
     and Seen*, Newsletter of Swedenborg Society, no. 32, Summer
     2010.

10 Peter Ackroyd, *Blake* (London: Sinclair-Stevenson, 1995).

11 Aidan Andrew Dun, *Vale Royal* (Uppingham: Goldmark, 1995).

12 William Blake, 'London', in *Songs of Innocence and Of Experience* (1789-94).

13 Joseph Conrad, *Heart of Darkness*, in *Youth: A Narrative and Two Other Stories* (Edinburgh and London: William Blackwood and Sons, 1902).

14 Rachel Lichtenstein, *Diamond Street: The Hidden World of Hatton Garden* (London: Hamish Hamilton, 2012).

15 William Blake, *Jerusalem, The Emanation of The Giant Albion* (1804-20), plate 5, ll. 1-3 and plate 84, ll. 1-3.

16 Paul Willetts, *Fear and Loathing in Fitzrovia: The Strange Lives of Julian Maclaren-Ross* (Stockport: Dewi Lewis, 2005).

17 Carol Williams, 'Moving', in Iain Sinclair (ed.), *London, City of Disappearances* (London: Hamish Hamilton, 2006).

18 Aidan Andrew Dun, *The Brill* (2012).

19 Emanuel Swedenborg, *The Last Judgment (Posthumous)*, tr. John Whitehead (London: Swedenborg Society, 1934).

20 Thomas Boyle, *Black Swine in the Sewers of Hampstead* (Beneath the Surface of Victorian Sensationalism) (London: Hodder & Stoughton,1989).

21 Allen Fisher, *Place* (London: Reality Street Editions, 2005).

22 Bill Griffiths, 'The Abbey', in *Fire*, no. 10, January 2000.

23 Allen Fisher, *Place* (London: Reality Street Editions, 2005).

24 *Hackney, That Rose-Red Empire* (London: Hamish Hamilton, 2009).

25 Ibid.

26 S Foster Damon, *A Blake Dictionary* (London: Thames and Hudson, 1973).